This Book
Belongs To:

Happy Galentine's Day

FIRST EDITION

Cupid
is
Stupid

my cat

is

my

valentine

yep
STILL
single

Why fall in
LOVE
when you can fall
ASLEEP

Team
No
valentine

Coffee is my

Valentine

galentine's
DAY SQUAD

I Love Me!

Single
AND
loving it

happy
SINGLES
awareness
DAY

february
14TH
JUST ANOTHER DAY!

At least my

dog loves me

in
LOVE
with
Myself

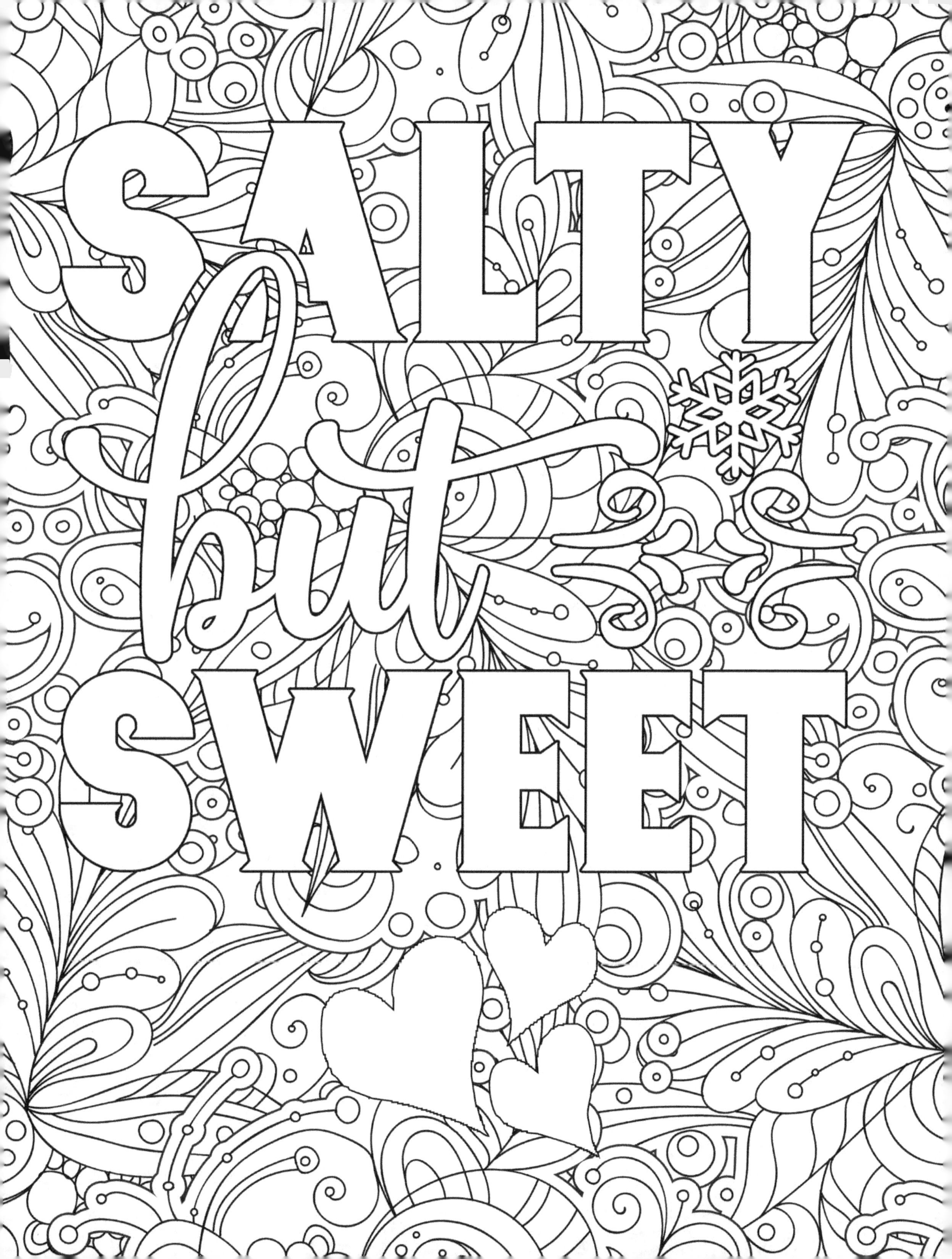
SALTY
but
SWEET

I HATE YOU THE LEAST

I believe in love at third beer

Valentines' day
SINGLE
and
fabulous

PIZZA IS MY
VALENTINE

YOU
are a good
reason to be
HAPPY

NO
CUPID
ZONE

WILL YOU BE MY
Valentine?
JUST KIDDING
I HATE
(everyone)

Be the reason someone smiles today

LOVE
with
all your
heart

BE
KIND

LOVE IS
in the air
try not to
BREATHE

HAPPY VALENTINES DAY
TO ME
I LOVE YOU

L♥VE
BITES

SINGLE
and
FABULOUS

FIND
Something
you love
and do it
FOREVER

LOVE
DISAPPOINTING
PIZZA
IS ETERNAL

www.ingramcontent.com/pod-product-compliance
Lightning Source LLC
Chambersburg PA
CBHW081320250726
48662CB00008B/2663
9798599160533